Coffee in Eastbourne

By

George G A Wensley

New Generation Publishing

About George G A Wensley

I was born to an English father and a Scottish mother and have lived all my life in the South East of England, apart from a brief eight month stay in Leicester.

The first ten years of my life were in Bexley Heath, mostly before the expansion of London, so I do love the county of Kent. My father's parents lived in Ramsgate, where we visited every month, so I got to see the open sea in all its majesty and its moods. There was always a competition to say the words *thallata! thallata!* The Greek for the sea! The sea! When the family visited Ramsgate.

The family alternated holidays between Scotland and France, usually under canvas or staying with relatives. The A68 road is a special road to us, as my mother's home sickness permeated into us, as we got closer to the border. There was a sense of magic as we crossed the border at Carter Bar.

In common with a lot of mankind I like to travel, I have been to France, Greece and Italy several times. Once only to Austria, Belgium, Canada, Germany and USA.

I like to travel and review places on TripAdvisor of which I have had thousands of reviews read, which was one of the inspirations to writing this small book.

From childhood, although I am dyslexic, I have always wanted to write or tell stories. Some of the books, slowly read, but read, were Wind in the Willows, The Hobbit and The Wizard of OZ.

I went to secondary school at a place near to Watford, where I got a love of Mathematics, bizarrely because I did not have to write. It was in the country side so, if you got bored with classes, you could look out of the window and observe nature. Like Earth in The Hitch Hikers Guide To The Galaxy, it was closed down due to its proximity to the, yet to be built M25 motorway. I got great comfort from reading, though.

I have two A levels in Maths and briefly attended Leicester Poly, where I learnt that my mother was dying of cancer. I did not complete the first year. I then did a lot of stores and office jobs for original engineering companies in the field of Construction and Public works machines. Due to a break in my hip I had to stop work and took the opportunity to do courses in IT and a Creative writing course that I completed. I have written two books and an Anthology, had a further hip replacement and am able to do light physical work now.

I have lived in Bexleyheath, Watford, Leicester, Kent, Rochester, Allhallows, Maidstone, Marden, Tonbridge and now live in Eastbourne.

In later life I travelled a lot to Eastbourne and fell in love with the place.

About the book

I intended to list and describe at least 50 places to buy coffee in Eastbourne, that I have visited and enjoyed, and to check the details with the owners or managers of the coffee shops. I have achieved most of these aims, but have had the opportunity to work in other areas, so I have had to edit some places out and stop the verification work. Those coffee shops that have a v in the author's comments have been verified that the owner / manager is happy with the content on their shops. Should you buy this book and recommend that your friends buy the book as well, I will be able to make a more comprehensive list of coffee shops in Eastbourne. It is my mission, but I do not think it will be impossible, with your help.

The coffee shops in this book could be at the station, the busy thorough fares, or an out of the way back street. There are coffee shops for all tastes in this book.

Other books by George

Text: Murder, a crime thriller, which is going through the process of being screened.

Devil's Gate, re-named as Queen's Bet the sequel to Text: Murder

Prose, Photos and Poems, a compendium of short stories, poems and photography.

All of these books are available on Amazon.

Index

About Eastbourne

Eastbourne is a lovely sea side town, which boasts a lot of sunshine. There is so much to do in Eastbourne. It has a hand full of theatres, cinemas, art galleries, mini fun parks, historical sites, hotels and much more.

Here are a few places of interest:-

Beachy Head, Burling Gap, Eastbourne Bandstand, Towner Art Gallery, Museum of Shops, Redoubt Fortress, Eastbourne Pier, The Wish Tower and the Broad Walk Promenade.

Some useful websites and Facebook pages:-

coffeeineastbourne.co.uk

https://www.eastbournetheatres.co.uk

www.visiteastbourne.com

www.tripadvisor.co.uk/Attractions-g190722-Acctivities-

www.Ita.org.uk/major-events/aegon-international-eastbourne

www.eastbourne.gov.uk/visitors

www.wyntercon.com

Events in Eastbourne:

International Tennis June

Airbourne August

Winter con November

Plus there are regular events all around Eastbourne visit some of the websites in the previous page.

Coffee Beans

All our coffee is imported to the UK and Eastbourne. There are a surprising amount of countries that supply coffee beans to us. In the past that led to exploitation of coffee bean suppliers, which led to the fair trade organizations being established. There are a variety of ways of sourcing coffee beans depending on the coffee shop, whether it is a small shop or multinational corporation. Most of the coffee shop owners and managers that I have spoken to, take a pride in their coffee, the fact that they, or their employers take time to source their coffee responsibly and take an interest in the whole supply chain.

Coffee shops beginning with A

Name of premises	AMT		
Address	Terminus Station		
Website	http://amtcoffee.co.uk		
Contact	01323730878 07762497916		
Loyalty card			
Drink in	Yes	Drink out	Yes
Coffee description	Espresso machine coffee served with an ice cube if too hot		
Fair Trade Coffee			
wifi	Station		
Devise charging facilities	No		
Tables outside	Yes	Covered	Yes
Food	Snacks and pre-prepared sandwiches		
Cakes			
Baby changing facilities	No	Child's chair	No
Owner / Manager's Comment			
Author's comment	A good place to wait for the train or pick up a coffee before boarding the train. You can see the departures board from the seating area.		
Opening times	5:30 to 19:00 Sat 6:00 Sun 6:30		

Name of premises	Aroma cafe		
Address 54	Oklynge Road, Old Town, BN21 1PR.		
Website			
Contact	01323640263		
Loyalty card			
Drink in	Yes	Drink out	Yes
Coffee description	A varied selections of speciality filter coffee, specially blended.		
Fair Trade Coffee	Yes		
wifi			
Devise charging facilities			
Tables outside	yes	Covered	Yes
Food	A range of snacks and meals, at competitive prices, the fish is caught locally.		
Cakes	Yes		
Baby changing facilities		Child's chair	Yes
Owner / Manager's Comment			
Author's comment	A very nice independent coffee shop, with an old world ambiance and friendly service. I can recommend the food.		
Opening times			

Coffee shops beginning with B

Name of premises	Bella's Secrete House of stunning cakes
Address	Enterprise Centre, Station Parade, Eastbourne, BN21 1BD
Website	
Contact	Tel 07718093794 email bella@bellassecret.co.uk
Loyalty card	Yes
Drink in	Yes Drink out Yes
Coffee description	Italian style coffee, blended by the owner, from a unique selection of South American beans.
Fair Trade Coffee	No
wifi	Yes
Devise charging facilities	Yes
Tables outside	No Covered No
Food	No
Cakes	Yes, they specialize in cakes, make them on site, supply them to weddings and are the preferred wedding supplier to The Grand Hotel.
Baby changing facilities	Not on this site but available at the centre Child's chair No
Owner / Manager's Comment	
Author's comment	Very pleasant environment, you can watch cakes being made or site in comfy chairs and enjoy a coffee and cake. V
Opening times	9 tom 5 Sundays 10 to 4

Name of premises	Bella's Cafe
Address	Terminus Station Concourse, Terminus Road BN21 3QJ
Website	bellassecret.co.uk
Contact	Tel 07718093794
Loyalty card	Yes
Drink in	Yes Drink out Yes
Coffee description	Italian style coffee, blended to the owners specifications from beans from South America.
Fair Trade Coffee	No
wifi	Yes
Devise charging facilities	Yes
Tables outside	Yes Covered Yes
Food	Sandwiches and snacks
Cakes	The cakes are homemade and range from cup cakes to slices of cakes. They even make wedding cakes.
Baby changing facilities	No Child's chair No
Owner / Manager's Comment	
Author's comment	A place to relax before alighting to a train, or just relax. V
Opening times	5 to 7 weekends 8 to 7

Name of premises	Beanzz		
Address	39 Grove Road, Eastbourne, East Sussex BN21 4TX		
Website	www.beanzzcoffee.co.uk		
Contact			
Loyalty card			
Drink in	Yes	Drink out	Yes
Coffee description	Nice coffee		
Fair Trade Coffee	Yes		
wifi	Yes		
Devise charging facilities			
Tables outside	Yes	Covered	Yes
Food	snacks and lunch time food.		
Cakes	Yes		
Baby changing facilities		Child's chair	
Owner / Manager's Comment			
Author's comment	A nice place to meet people at the wooden kitchen tables or sit in a comfy chair.		
Opening times	Mon to Fri 8:00 AM to 4:00 PM		
	Sat 9:00 to 4:00 PM Sun 10:00 to 3:00 PM		

Name of premises	Black Cat		
Address	Meads Shops		
Website			
Contact			
Loyalty card			
Drink in	Yes	Drink out	Yes
Coffee description	Espresso Machine		
Fair Trade Coffee	Yes		
wifi			
Devise charging facilities			
Tables outside	Yes	Covered	Yes
Food	Various snacks and light meals		
Cakes	Yes		
Baby changing facilities		Child's chair	Yes
Owner / Manager's Comment			
Author's comment	This 'place is off the beaten track and has an old world charm, I can recommend the toasted cheese sandwiches.		
Opening times			

Name of premises	Broadwalk Cafe		
Address	4 Lower Parade, Eastbourne East Sussex BN21 3AD		
Website			
Contact	01424810129		
Loyalty card	No		
Drink in	Yes	Drink out	Yes
Coffee description	Italian style coffee		
Fair Trade Coffee	Yes		
wifi	No		
Devise charging facilities	Yes		
Tables outside	Yes	Covered	Yes
Food	Snacks		
Cakes	Yes		
Baby changing facilities	No	Child's chair	Yes
Owner / Manager's Comment			
Author's comment	I have used this place for a while and always received a warm welcome. The prices are competitive. V		
Opening times	7:30 AM to 5:30 PM Winter 7:30 to Late in the summer.		

Coffee shops beginning with C

Name of premises	Coffee Republic		
Address	Terminus Road		
Website			
Contact			
Loyalty card			
Drink in	Yes	Drink out	Yes
Coffee description	Espresso Machine		
Fair Trade Coffee	Yes		
wifi	Yes		
Devise charging facilities	Yes		
Tables outside	Yes	Covered	Yes
Food	Light snacks		
Cakes	Yes		
Baby changing facilities		Child's chair	Yes
Owner / Manager's Comment			
Author's comment	Popular coffee shop on the main shopping street of Eastbourne, comfy chairs inside or enjoy a coffee outside.		
Opening times			

Coffee shops beginning with D

Name of premises	Dickens's Tea Rooms		
Address	South Road		
Website			
Contact			
Loyalty card			
Drink in	Yes	Drink out	Yes
Coffee description	Made on site.		
Fair Trade Coffee			
wifi			
Devise charging facilities			
Tables outside		Covered	
Food	Primarily tea rooms, so the food is of that type.		
Cakes			
Baby changing facilities		Child's chair	Yes
Owner / Manager's Comment			
Author's comment	The rooms are decorated with Dickens memorabilia. As I used to live in Rochester it brings back memories.		
Opening times			

Coffee shops beginning with E

Name of premises	Costas		
Address	Eastbourne General Hospital		
Website			
Contact			
Loyalty card			
Drink in	Yes	Drink out	Yes
Coffee description	Espresso machine		
Fair Trade Coffee	Yes		
wifi			
Devise charging facilities			
Tables outside	No	Covered	
Food	Light healthy snacks		
Cakes			
Baby changing facilities	Yes	Child's chair	Yes
Owner / Manager's Comment			
Author's comment	A nice place at the entrance of Eastbourne District General Hospital to wait for an appointment.		
Opening times			

Name of premises   Eucalyptus and Paprika

Address   South Road

Website

Contact

Loyalty card

Drink in   Yes   Drink out Yes

Coffee description   Espresso coffee machine

Fair Trade Coffee

wifi

Devise charging facilities

Tables outside   Covered

Food   Yes they specialise in Hungarian food I can recommend the goulash.

Cakes   Yes

Baby changing facilities   Child's chair Yes

Owner / Manager's Comment

Author's comment   An interesting shop, that Hungarian ex pats go to.

Opening times

Coffee shops beginning with F

Name of premises	Favaloso
Address	19 - 25 Carlisle Road, Eastbourne
Website	No
Contact	
Loyalty card	No
Drink in	Yes Drink out Yes
Coffee description	Italian coffee made in a coffee machine with a delicate flavour.
Fair Trade Coffee	Yes
wifi	No
Devise charging facilities	No
Tables outside	Yes Covered No
Food	A range of English and Italian meals and snacks at competitive prices.
Cakes	A range of cakes.
Baby changing facilities	Yes Child's chair Yes
Owner / Manager's Comment	Comment Italian Gelato (ice cream) sold here!
Author's comment	I have used this cafe restaurant at different times of year, the service, quality of produce and value is always very good! I have reviewed Favaloso on trip advisor, where there have been some famous names who have raved about this establishment. V
Opening times	8.45 Am to 7 PM Depending on what's on at the Theatres or 6 PM.

Name of premises	Fiesta Bistro		
Address	6 Grove Road BN21 4TJ		
Website			
Contact			
Loyalty card			
Drink in	Yes	Drink out	Yes
Coffee description			
Fair Trade Coffee			
wifi			
Devise charging facilities			
Tables outside	Yes	Covered	Yes
Food	Bistro type food		
Cakes			
Baby changing facilities		Child's chair	
Owner / Manager's Comment			
Author's comment			
Opening times			

Name of premises	Fusciardi's
Address	30 Marine Parade, BN22 7AY
Website	www.fusciardiicecreams.co.uk
Contact	
Loyalty card	Yes
Drink in	Yes Drink out Yes
Coffee description	Made with a professional Italian coffee machine and have the facility to vary the strength of the coffee.
Fair Trade Coffee	
wifi	
Devise charging facilities	
Tables outside	Yes Covered Yes
Food	Yes. There is a range of Italian and English food and of course homemade gelato! (Ice cream)
Cakes	
Baby changing facilities	Child's chair Yes
Owner / Manager's Comment	2017 will be the 50th anniversary of Fusciardi's
Author's comment	I have used this coffee shop for over 10 years and will always come back, due to the excellent service and produce! V
Opening times	9AM to 5PM in the winter 9AM until late in the summer.

Coffee shops beginning with G

Name of premises	Giorgio's		
Address			
Website			
Contact			
Loyalty card	Yes		
Drink in	Yes	Drink out	Yes
Coffee description	Espresso Machine		
Fair Trade Coffee			
wifi			
Devise charging facilities			
Tables outside	Yes	Covered	Yes
Food	Light snacks		
Cakes	Yes		
Baby changing facilities		Child's chair	Yes
Owner / Manager's Comment			
Author's comment	A nice place in the centre of town.		
Opening times			

Name of premises	Greggs		
Address	ARNDALE CENTRE		
Website			
Contact			
Loyalty card			
Drink in	Yes	Drink out	Yes
Coffee description	Coffee machine		
Fair Trade Coffee			
wifi			
Devise charging facilities			
Tables outside	No	Covered	No
Food	Yes I recommend the sausage rolls		
Cakes			
Baby changing facilities		Child's chair	
Owner / Manager's Comment			
Author's comment			
Opening times			

Coffee shops beginning with H

Name of premises	Holywell Tea Rooms		
Address	Broad Walk		
Website			
Contact			
Loyalty card			
Drink in	Yes	Drink out	Yes
Coffee description	Espresso Machine		
Fair Trade Coffee			
wifi			
Devise charging facilities			
Tables outside	Yes	Covered	Yes
Food	Light snacks and meals		
Cakes	Yes		
Baby changing facilities		Child's chair	Yes
Owner / Manager's Comment			
Author's comment	Holywell is one of my favourite places in Eastbourne. After a walk along the Broadwalk no better place to have a sheltered rest.		
Opening times			

Coffee shops beginning with I

Name of premises	IL Gusto		
Address	Grove Road		
Website			
Contact			
Loyalty card			
Drink in	Yes	Drink out	Yes
Coffee description			
Fair Trade Coffee	Yes		
wifi	Yes		
Devise charging facilities	Yes		
Tables outside	Yes	Covered	Yes
Food	Homemade Italian Food		
Cakes			
Baby changing facilities		Child's chair	Yes
Owner / Manager's Comment			
Author's comment			
Opening times			

Coffee shops beginning with J

Name of premises	Jasper Wood
Address	19 Cornfield terrace BN21 4NS
Website	jasperwood.co.uk
	on Facebook as well.
Contact	
Loyalty card	No
Drink in	Yes Drink out Yes
Coffee description	Peruvian specially blended and supplied to the owners specifications.
Fair Trade Coffee	Yes
wifi	Yes
Devise charging facilities	Yes
Tables outside	No Covered No
Food	Light snacks, rolls and salads
Cakes	Yes
Baby changing facilities	N o Child's chair No
Owner / Manager's Comment	We offer a relaxing atmosphere.
Author's comment	I have used this coffee for many years and had a relaxing time. I have even bought some collectables here. Conversations groups welcome. v
Opening times	Closed Mondays and Sundays. 8:30 to 4:30

Name of premises	Jocelyn's		
Address	Business Centre		
Website			
Contact			
Loyalty card			
Drink in	Yes	Drink out	Yes
Coffee description	Italian style coffee		
Fair Trade Coffee	Yes		
wifi	Yes		
Devise charging facilities	Yes		
Tables outside	Yes (but in centre so no smoking)	Covered	Yes
Food	Light snacks and meals		
Cakes	Yes		
Baby changing facilities		Child's chair	
Owner / Manager's Comment			
Author's comment			
Opening times			

Coffee shops beginning with K

Name of premises	Kiosk The		
Address	Meads		
Website			
Contact			
Loyalty card			
Drink in	Yes	Drink out	Yes
Coffee description	Espresso machine		
Fair Trade Coffee			
wifi			
Devise charging facilities			
Tables outside	Yes	Covered	Yes
Food	Light snacks and ice cream		
Cakes			
Baby changing facilities		Child's chair	
Owner / Manager's Comment			
Author's comment	This is the last stop before the walk to Beachy Head. It is dog friendly and is open all year round.		
Opening times			

Coffee shops beginning with M

Name of premises	McDonalds		
Address	Terminus Road		
Website	24		
Contact			
Loyalty card			
Drink in	Yes	Drink out	Yes
Coffee description	Corporation standard.		
Fair Trade Coffee			
wifi	Yes		
Devise charging facilities	Yes		
Tables outside		Covered	
Food	Yes the usual McDonalds Fair.		
Cakes			
Baby changing facilities		Child's chair	Yes
Owner / Manager's Comment			
Author's comment	A good place the grab some food, any time of day or night. Handy for the buses.		
Opening times			

Coffee shops beginning with M

Name of premises	Millie's Cookies		
Address	Arndale centre		
Website			
Contact			
Loyalty card			
Drink in	Yes	Drink out	Yes
Coffee description			
Fair Trade Coffee			
wifi			
Devise charging facilities			
Tables outside	Yes (but in the Arndale Centre so no smoking)	Covered	Yes
Food	Yes		
Cakes	Yes		
Baby changing facilities		Child's chair	
Owner / Manager's Comment			
Author's comment			
Opening times			

Name of premises	Muffin Break		
Address	Arndale Centre		
Website			
Contact			
Loyalty card			
Drink in	Yes	Drink out	Yes
Coffee description			
Fair Trade Coffee			
wifi			
Devise charging facilities			
Tables outside		Covered	
Food	Yes		
Cakes	Yes		
Baby changing facilities		Child's chair	
Owner / Manager's Comment			
Author's comment			
Opening times			

Coffee shops beginning with N

Name of premises	Nelson's
Address	4 Terminus Road, Eastbourne, East Sussex, BN21 3LP
Website	nelsoncoffee.co.uk
Contact	
Loyalty card	Yes
Drink in	Yes Drink out Yes
Coffee description	A variety of differently flavoured coffees, Americano, Lattes and Espressos served in small medium and large.
Fair Trade Coffee	Yes
wifi	Yes
Devise charging facilities	Yes
Tables outside	Yes Covered Yes
Food	There are a variety of, snacks, sandwiches, rolls, scones and meals, home produced with local ingredients like Sussex Jam.
Cakes	Cakes are home produced.
Baby changing facilities	Child's chair Yes
Owner / Manager's Comment	
Author's comment	Nelson's is a coffee shop that I have visited regularly, It is run by the owners who are friendly and efficient. The staff are well trained and friendly. V
Opening times	

Name of premises	Caffe Nero's
Address	138/140 Terminus Road, BN21 3AN
Website	
Contact	01323417977
Loyalty card	Yes
Drink in	Yes Drink out Yes
Coffee description	All Nero's have a bespoke coffee machine that provide an excellent coffee.
Fair Trade Coffee	Yes Nero's works with farmers to help them out.
wifi	Yes
Devise charging facilities	Yes
Tables outside	Yes Covered Yes
Food	Light snacks and Panini's
Cakes	Muffins cakes and slices of cakes.
Baby changing facilities	Yes Child's chair Yes
Owner / Manager's Comment	
Author's comment	My favourite coffee shop franchise is Nero's, I have had at least 1 cup of coffee a week at Nero's for the last 11 years. Comfy chairs, nice Italian decor, of course good coffee and snacks. V
Opening times	Monday to Friday 7 to 6 Saturday 7.30 6.30 Sunday 8 to 6

Coffee shops beginning with P

Name of premises	Patisserie Valerie		
Address	Terminus Road		
Website			
Contact			
Loyalty card			
Drink in	Yes	Drink out	Yes
Coffee description			
Fair Trade Coffee			
wifi			
Devise charging facilities			
Tables outside		Covered	
Food			
Cakes			
Baby changing facilities		Child's chair	Yes
Owner / Manager's Comment			
Author's comment			
Opening times			

Name of premises   Pianta Del Caffe

Address   Terminus Road

Website

Contact

Loyalty card

Drink in   Yes   Drink out   Yes

Coffee description

Fair Trade Coffee

wifi

Devise charging facilities

Tables outside   Covered

Food

Cakes

Baby changing facilities   Child's chair

Owner / Manager's
Comment

Author's comment

Opening times

Coffee shops beginning with R

Name of premises	The Redoubt Cafe		
Address	Just off the Eastern Broadwalk		
Website			
Contact			
Loyalty card			
Drink in	Yes	Drink out	Yes
Coffee description	Espresso machine		
Fair Trade Coffee			
wifi			
Devise charging facilities			
Tables outside	Yes	Covered	Yes
Food	Light snacks		
Cakes	Yes		
Baby changing facilities		Child's chair	Yes
Owner / Manager's Comment			
Author's comment	In the grounds of the redoubt fortress.		
Opening times			

Coffee shops beginning with S

Name of premises	Starbucks		
Address			
Website			
Contact			
Loyalty card			
Drink in	Yes	Drink out	Yes
Coffee description			
Fair Trade Coffee	Yes		
wifi	Yes		
Devise charging facilities	Yes		
Tables outside	Yes	Covered	Yes
Food			
Cakes			
Baby changing facilities		Child's chair	Yes
Owner / Manager's Comment			
Author's comment			
Opening times			

Coffee shops beginning with S

Name of premises	Subway		
Address	Eastbourne Terminus Station		
Website			
Contact			
Loyalty card			
Drink in	Yes	Drink out	Yes
Coffee description			
Fair Trade Coffee			
wifi			
Devise charging facilities			
Tables outside	Yes	Covered	Yes
Food			
Cakes			
Baby changing facilities		Child's chair	
Owner / Manager's Comment			
Author's comment			
Opening times			

Coffee shops beginning with T

Name of premises	Tchibo coffee		
Address			
Website	www.tchibo-coffee.co.uk		
Contact			
Loyalty card	Yes		
Drink in	Yes	Drink out	Yes
Coffee description			
Fair Trade Coffee	Yes		
wifi	Yes		
Devise charging facilities	Yes		
Tables outside	Yes	Covered	Yes
Food			
Cakes			
Baby changing facilities		Child's chair	Yes
Owner / Manager's Comment			
Author's comment			
Opening times			

Name of premises	Towner Gallery		
Address			
Website			
Contact			
Loyalty card			
Drink in	Yes	Drink out	Yes
Coffee description			
Fair Trade Coffee			
wifi			
Devise charging facilities			
Tables outside	No	Covered	No
Food	Yes		
Cakes			
Baby changing facilities		Child's chair	
Owner / Manager's Comment			
Author's comment			
Opening times			

Coffee shops beginning with U

Name of premises	Urban Ground		
Address			
Website			
Contact			
Loyalty card			
Drink in	Yes	Drink out	Yes
Coffee description			
Fair Trade Coffee	Yes		
wifi	Yes		
Devise charging facilities	Yes		
Tables outside	Yes	Covered	Yes
Food			
Cakes			
Baby changing facilities		Child's chair	Yes
Owner / Manager's Comment			
Author's comment			
Opening times			

Coffee shops beginning with V

Name of premises	Vickerys		
Address	Terminus Road		
Website			
Contact			
Loyalty card			
Drink in	Yes	Drink out	Yes
Coffee description			
Fair Trade Coffee	Yes		
wifi	Yes		
Devise charging facilities	Yes		
Tables outside	Yes	Covered	Yes
Food			
Cakes			
Baby changing facilities		Child's chair	Yes
Owner / Manager's Comment			
Author's comment			
Opening times			

End note

I hope you have enjoyed this book and have found it useful. My thanks to all the coffee shops in Eastbourne. I am sorry if I haven't been to your shop, if this book is a success I will review your shop. My Thanks to my publishers.

www.ingramcontent.com/pod-product-compliance
Lightning Source LLC
Chambersburg PA
CBHW051127250726
48655CB00007B/2923